The Ultimate
Christmas Coloring Book
for Kids

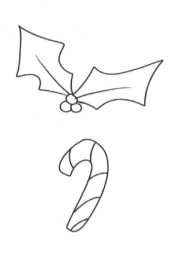

www.feelhappybooks.com

Feel Happy Books are a group of talented artists that share a passion for creating fun and relaxing kids coloring books.

Please do write to us and give us your feedback, we genuinely would love to hear from you. What coloring books would you like us to do next?

Email us to ask if we have any special offers just for you on our other coloring books. Our email is help@feelhappybooks.com

We also want to post your finished artwork on our own website and Facebook page so share it with the world...

www.feelhappybooks.com
www.facebook.com/feelhappybooks

Copyright and Trademarks

This book belongs to:

_____

Your FREE Gift!!!

As a special thank you, we have a bonus coloring ebook which you can download to your computer and print.

Just email us at mj@thelearningbugs.com to ask for your FREE Learning Bugs mini ebook.

Please Can You Help Us?

Leaving a helpful review and rating on the website where you bought this book means more children can discover our wonderful books!

How to Color This Book...

Put a sheet of paper or card behind each page in case the color comes through.

Have you seen our other coloring books featuring The Learning Bugs? You can find them at all good online book retailers."

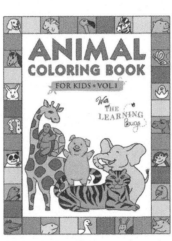

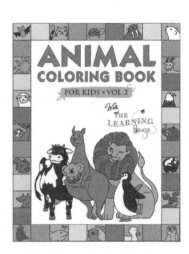

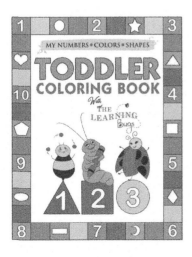

Made in the USA
Middletown, DE
29 November 2020